WELDER PRACTICE QUESTIONS

Welder Practice Questions
Similar to Red Seal or AWS
Welder Exam

Copyright 2022 Complete Test Preparation Inc. All Rights Reserved.

No part of this book may be reproduced or transferred in any form or by any means, graphic, electronic, or mechanical, including photocopying, recording, web distribution, taping, or by any information storage retrieval system, without the written permission of the author.

Notice: Complete Test Preparation Inc. makes every reasonable effort to obtain from reliable sources accurate, complete, and timely information about the tests covered in this book. Nevertheless, changes can be made in the tests or the administration of the tests at any time and Complete Test Preparation Inc. makes no representation or warranty, either expressed or implied as to the accuracy, timeliness, or completeness of the information contained in this book. Complete Test Preparation Inc. make no representations or warranties of any kind, express or implied, about the completeness, accuracy, reliability, suitability or availability with respect to the information contained in this document for any purpose. Any reliance you place on such information is therefore strictly at your own risk.

The author(s) shall not be liable for any loss incurred as a consequence of the use and application, directly or indirectly, of any information presented in this work. Sold with the understanding, the author is not engaged in rendering professional services or advice. If advice or expert assistance is required, the services of a competent professional should be sought.

The company, product and service names used in this publication are for identification purposes only. All trademarks and registered trademarks are the property of their respective owners. Complete Test Preparation Inc. is not affiliated with any educational institution.

We strongly recommend that students check with exam providers for up-to-date information regarding test content.

Complete Test Preparation Inc. is not affiliated with the Canada Red Seal Program, who are not involved in the production of, and do not endorse this publication. Questions are presented for skill practice only.

ISBN-13: 9781772453997

Version 8.5 February 2023

ABOUT COMPLETE TEST PREPARATION INC.

Why Us?
The Complete Test Preparation Team has been publishing high quality study materials since 2005, with a catalogue of over 145 titles, in English, French and Chinese, as well as curriculum for all levels.

To keep up with the industry changes, we update everything all the time!

And the best part?
With every purchase, you're helping people all over the world improve themselves and their education. So thank you in advance for supporting this mission with us! Together, we are truly making a difference in the lives of those often forgotten by the system.

Charities that we support -
https://www.test-preparation.ca/charities-and-non-profits/

You have definitely come to the right place.
If you want to spend your valuable study time where it will help you the most - we've got you covered today and tomorrow.

Published by
Complete Test Preparation Inc.
Victoria BC Canada

Visit us on the web at https://www.test-preparation.ca
Printed in the USA

FEEDBACK

We welcome your feedback. Email us at feedback@test-preparation.ca with your comments and suggestions. We carefully review all suggestions and often incorporate reader suggestions into upcoming versions. As a Print on Demand Publisher, we update our products frequently.

https://www.facebook.com/CompleteTestPreparation/

https://www.youtube.com/user/MrTestPreparation

Contents

6	**Getting Started**	
9	**Common Occupational Skills**	
	Answer Key	16
24	**Preparation and Fabrication of Components**	
	Answer Key	36
42	**Welding Processes**	
	Answer Key	51
44	**Shielded Metal and Gas Metal Arc Welding**	
	Answer Key	68
72	**Cutting and Gouging**	
	Answer Key	80
90	**Conclusion**	
93	**Online Test Prep Resources**	

Getting Started

CONGRATULATIONS! By deciding to take the Welder test, you have taken the first step toward a great future! Of course, there is no point in taking this important examination unless you intend to do your best to earn the highest grade you possibly can. That means getting yourself organized and discovering the best approaches, methods and strategies to master the material. Yes, that will require real effort and dedication, but if you are willing to focus your energy and devote the study time necessary, before you know it you will be opening that letter of acceptance.

We know that taking on a new endeavour can be scary, and it is easy to feel unsure of where to begin. That's where we come in. This study guide is designed to help you improve your test-taking skills, show you a few tricks of the trade and increase both your competency and confidence.

What is on a Welder Certification Test?

Common Occupational Skills

   Questions on tools and equipment maintenance.

   Questions on material handling equipment.

   Workplace safety.

   Work organization.

   Routine activities.

Preparation and fabrication of welding components.

    Layout performance.

    Component fabrication.

Cutting and Gouging

    Use of tools and equipment for grinding and non-thermal cutting.

    Oxy-fuel gas cutting (OFC) for gouging and cutting.

    Plasma arc cutting (PAC) in cutting and gouging.

    Air carbon arc cutting (CAC-A) in cutting and gouging.

Welding processes

    Shielded metal arc welding processes

    Gas metal arc welding, metal cored arc welding, and flux cored arc welding processes.

    Gas tungsten arc welding processes.

    Submerged arc welding.

The questions below are not the same as you will find on a welding test - that would be too easy! And nobody knows what the questions will be and they change all the time. Below are general questions that cover the same subject areas as most welding tests. So, while the format and exact wording of the questions may differ slightly, and change from year to year, if you can answer the questions below, you will have no problem with your welding test.

For the best results, take these practice test questions as if it were the real exam. Set aside time when you will not be disturbed, and a location that is quiet and free of distractions. Read the instructions carefully, read each question carefully, and answer to the best of your ability.

Use the bubble answer sheets provided. When you have completed the Practice Questions, check your answer against the Answer Key and read the explanation provided.

Do not attempt more than one set of practice test questions in one day. After completing the first practice test, wait two or three days before attempting the second set of questions.

Common Occupational Skills

Common Occupational Skills include:

- Questions on tools and equipment maintenance.
- Questions on material handling equipment.
- Questions on workplace safety.
- Questions on work organization.
- Questions on routine trade activities.

Answer Sheet

1. A B C D   11. A B C D
2. A B C D   12. A B C D
3. A B C D   13. A B C D
4. A B C D   14. A B C D
5. A B C D   15. A B C D
6. A B C D   16. A B C D
7. A B C D   17. A B C D
8. A B C D   18. A B C D
9. A B C D
10. A B C D

1. What you should NOT wear for safety during oxy-fuel gas welding?

   a. Tight fitting shirts
   b. Loose fitting shirts
   c. A helmet
   d. Boots

2. Which of the following will avoid electric shocks in electrical arc welding?

   a. Insulated gloves
   b. Insulated boots
   c. Dry insulated material in a confined space
   d. All of the above

3. Which of the following is NOT a safety measure for a gas welding location?

   a. Hoses clear
   b. Clearly marked 'hot' work
   c. Clean and clear floor
   d. None of the above

4. When moving a gas cylinder _____

   a. Lift using the protective CO2 valve cap
   b. Keep the regulator in place
   c. Secure it to a wheeled hand cart
   d. Use grease if moving into a tight space

5. Which parts of gas regulators do NOT require periodic maintenance?

   a. Filters
   b. Regulator seats
   c. Pressure gauges
   d. Cylinder base

6. Which is the safest cloth for use in a welding shop?

    a. Silk
    b. Leather
    c. Cotton
    d. Nylon

7. Which of the following is a daily maintenance check for gas welding?

    a. Check the hose pipe for leakage
    b. Check blow pipe tips for carbon or slag
    c. Apply solution to suspected leaks daily
    d. All of the Above

8. Which of the following is a daily maintenance check for arc welding?

    a. Check for damage in electrical cables
    b. Check hoses, torches, electrodes, cylinders and connections
    c. Check power controller
    d. All of the Above

9. Which of the following is a control check for concentration and exposure to fumes in arc welding?

    a. Substitution
    b. Limiting the period of exposure
    c. Work methods
    d. All of the above

10. Which ventilation methods collect fumes at source and direct them away from the work area?

    a. Natural ventilation

    b. General exhaust ventilation

    c. Local exhaust ventilation

    d. Local dispersion ventilation

11. What is the best eye protection for arc welding?

    a. Helmet/Face shield

    b. Sunglasses

    c. Mask

    d. Clear glass

12. Arc welding equipment should never be operated

    a. Standing in a wet area

    b. In a poorly lighted area

    c. When someone is standing nearby

    d. In a confined space without proper ventilation

13. Which of the following are safety precautions for working in a confined space?

    a. A lifeline must be attached

    b. All leads and hoses are to be kept clear of the floor, dampness and falling metal sparks. Circular vessels must be prevented from rolling

    c. Oxygen should never be used for dusting down or any purpose other than the oxy-flame

    d. All of the Above

14. Which of the following are safety precautions for working in hazardous locations?

a. Work must be carried out in accordance with the provisions of the hot work permit

b. Always examine the possibility of removing the work to a safe area

c. Always check behind walls, partitions, bulkheads etc, to ensure safety in adjoining areas

d. All of the Above

15. When moving a gas cylinder,

a. Lift using the protective valve cap

b. Secure to a wheeled hand cart

c. Use grease if it must be fitted into tight space

d. Keep the regulator in place

16. What steps should be taken if an acetylene cylinder leaks?

a. Shut off the valve if possible

b. Take the cylinder into the open air

c. Cool with water

d. All of the above

17. What are some short-term symptoms of 'arc eye' or 'weld flash?'

a. Dry eyes

b. Blindness

c. Extreme eye pain, nausea, headache

d. Infection, conjunctivitis, excessive wrinkling

18. What is the effect of a low current electrical shock?

    a. Loss of balance

    b. A mild burn at the contact area

    c. Loss of consciousness

    d. Extreme burn on the skin

Answer Key

1. B
Loose fitting shirts

• Safety clothing is essential working with welding equipment. This includes:

• general fabrication

• welding

• near machinery

• on scaffolding

• Safety clothing includes, heavy clothing that does not have pockets, properly secured, (buttoned down or tight fitting) so lose shirt or pant cuffs, baggy clothes, or sleeves do not get caught in moving parts.

• Proper Clothing includes:

• Sleeves rolled down and buttoned

• Heavy pants without cuffs and fire resistant

• Sturdy leather shoes or work boots (spark resistant, steel toe)

• Leather gloves and apron

• Non-flammable hat

• Leather cape or jacket

• Eye protection

• Ear protection

2. D
All of the above

Depending on the severity, an electric shock can cause minor tingling, or in more extreme cases, muscle spasms, or paralysis and in extreme cases death.

Gloves

Dry gloves, preferably leather, in good repair should be worn when handling equipment, particularly when changing electrodes.

Footwear

Footwear should be insulated, dry, and in good condition. Steel toe is preferred.

Equipment

Welding equipment should be fully insulated in working condition. Do not attempt repairs yourself!

Contacts

Select appropriate contacts that are tight and clean and close to the welding site.

Supply

Keep primary electrical supply circuits short. Do not attempt repairs yourself.

3. B
Mark work that is hot

4. C
When moving a gas cylinder, secure it to a wheeled hand cart.

Cylinder Safety and Handling

General safety

> 1. Keep all empty or full cylinders separated, (e.g. fuel gas, oxidizing gas, inert gas) and in an unlocked secure storage areas. This must be away from radiators, furnaces, other sources of heat and electrical circuits, and from direct sunlight.

2. Close valves of empty cylinders to keep water or contamination out.

3. Never tamper with or alter cylinder numbers, marking or colour coding.

4. Never try to refill a cylinder or try to mix gases in a cylinder.

5. Never use a cylinder or its contents for anything other than its intended purpose.

6. Keep oil, grease and all hydrocarbons away from cylinders. Keep them clean!

7. Make sure cylinders are upright and secure, and protect cylinder valves from bumps, falls, falling objects and the weather.

8. Never allow anyone to strike an arc or tap any electric arc against any cylinder.

9. Never draw oxygen or acetylene from cylinders except through properly attached pressure regulators.

10. If valves cannot be opened by hand, do not use a hammer or wrench - notify the supplier.

11. Never use cylinders as supports or rollers.

12. Always remove regulators before moving cylinders, and make sure valves are closed tightly before removing regulator.

13. Open cylinder valves slowly.

14. Never open a cylinder valve more than 1½ (one and a half) turns.

5. B
Pressure gauges do not require periodic maintenance.

Regulator Maintenance

Filters: Regulators have metal filters located in the bull nose end of the inlet. This protects the regulator by preventing particles from clogging the passages or damaging the seat, helping to eliminate the cause of creep.

Regulator seats: If the seat is damaged, it must be replaced. Excessive creep is the main indication of a damaged seat. Damaged regulators should be referred to the manufacturer for repairs.

6. B
Leather is the safest cloth in a welding workshop

Besides leather, proper clothing includes:

- Sleeves rolled down and buttoned
- Heavy pants without cuffs and fire resistant
- Sturdy leather shoes or work boots (spark resistant, steel toe)
- Leather apron
- Leather gloves
- Non-flammable hat
- Leather cape or jacket
- Eye protection
- Ear protection

7. D
All of the above.

Daily check list for gas welding:

1) Pressure regulator, flash arrestor, hose pipe, should be checked daily

2) Oxygen and acetylene shutoff valve should be checked for leakage daily

3) Inspect gas piping and manifold if using

4) Avoid lubricating the regulator to contact cylinders

8. D
All of the above.

9. D
All of the above.

To ensure that the concentration of fumes and exposure to fumes is within safe limits, various controls can be applied.

Substitution Where practicable, a less dangerous material, consumable, process, or procedure can be substituted.

Limiting the period of exposure Limiting the time any one operator is exposed to excessive fume concentration is not the most desirable method, but sometimes may be the only practical solution.

Work methods Limiting the time any one operator is exposed to excessive fume concentration is not the most desirable method, but in some cases may be the only practical solution.

Ventilation This is the most common method of control and can be achieved by various means.

10. C
Local Exhaust Ventilation

Natural ventilation – in most workshops and open sites, the natural flow of air through open plan layouts and natural breeze is sufficient to disperse fumes.

General exhaust ventilation – this method is often used where the workshop does not have adequate natural ventilation.

Local exhaust ventilation – this method collects fumes at source and directs them away from the work area. The suction inlet should be as close as possible to the source. There are various types of local exhaust systems, each offering certain advantages and suited to different applications.

Local dispersion ventilation – in some cases, suitable ventilation can be obtained locally by fans which deflect and disperse the fumes away from the operator

11. A
Helmet / Face Shield.

Protection is needed for both the eyes and skin. For arc welding, a suitable welding helmet or face shield, fitted with the recommended filter is essential.

Recommended Filters for Manual Metal Arc Welding (MMAW)

Amperage	Shade No.
Up to 100	8
100 - 200	10
200 - 300	11
400 - 500	12
Over 400	13

Higher current density/open arc processes such as GTAW or GMAW require darker shade lenses for the same current.

12. A
Standing in a wet area

13. D
All of the above.

- The workspace must be adequately ventilated
- A lifeline must be attached
- A semi-skilled operator who is trained in rescue and resuscitation must be stationed at the manhole to continually monitor the workspace; to adjust oxy-acetylene gear and the welding machine, while continually observing the operator.
- All leads and hoses are to be kept clear of the floor, dampness and falling metal sparks. Circular vessels must be prevented from rolling.
- General tidiness and care are essential, equipment should not be allowed to contact hot work or sharp objects.

- Oxy-flame cutting equipment should not be left inside a confined space when not in use, and should always be lit by the assistant outside and then passed to the operator inside.

- Oxygen should never be used for dusting down or any purpose other than for the oxy-flame

14. D
All of the above.

Tips for working in hazardous locations:

- Always inspect work areas for possible hazards.
- Seek authorization before proceeding with cutting or welding if in doubt.
- Ensure you are working according to the terms of the hot work permit.
- Always examine the possibility of removing the work to a safe area. Insure proper maintenance and inspect the location of safety screens, doors or barriers.
- Watch for sparks and offcuts.
- Inspect adjoining areas, i.e. behind walls, partitions, bulkheads etc, to ensure safety.
- Do not work near storage batteries.

15. D
When moving a gas cylinder, secure it to a wheeled hand cart.

16. D
All of the above.

17. C
Short-term symptoms of 'arc eye' or 'weld flash' are extreme eye pain, nausea, headache

Welding flash (arc eye)

- In mild cases, use eye-drops and shade the eyes.

- In severe cases, loosely pad both eyes (cold may help) and get medical attention as soon as possible.

Hot particles in the eyes

- Cover BOTH victim's eyes, and seek medical attention as soon as possible.

- For chemical burns, (e.g. from acids, alkalis or similar liquids) wash immediately flush continuously for up to 20 minutes to remove chemicals from the eyes.

- Urgently seek medical help.

18. B
A low current electrical shock can cause a mild burn at the contact area.

Preparation and Fabrication of Components

The Preparation and Fabrication of Components section includes:

- Questions that involve layout performance.
- Questions on component fabrication.

Answer Sheet

	A	B	C	D	E		A	B	C	D	E
1	○	○	○	○	○	21	○	○	○	○	○
2	○	○	○	○	○	22	○	○	○	○	○
3	○	○	○	○	○	23	○	○	○	○	○
4	○	○	○	○	○	24	○	○	○	○	○
5	○	○	○	○	○	25	○	○	○	○	○
6	○	○	○	○	○						
7	○	○	○	○	○						
8	○	○	○	○	○						
9	○	○	○	○	○						
10	○	○	○	○	○						
11	○	○	○	○	○						
12	○	○	○	○	○						
13	○	○	○	○	○						
14	○	○	○	○	○						
15	○	○	○	○	○						
16	○	○	○	○	○						
17	○	○	○	○	○						
18	○	○	○	○	○						
19	○	○	○	○	○						
20	○	○	○	○	○						

1. Which of the following factors is NOT important for weldability:

    a. Melting point

    b. Coefficient of thermal expansion

    c. Boiling point

    d. Thermal conductivity

2. Which of the following joints do NOT need any preparation such as bevel angle, root gap or root face:

    a. Single-vee groove butt joint

    b. Square butt and double-flare lap joint

    c. Single bevel groove butt joint

    d. All of the above

3. When inspecting materials coming onto a work site, which of the following should be included in your inspection?

    a. size/dimensions

    b. Condition

    c. Type/specification

    d. All of the above

4. The criteria for pipe material inspection includes:

    a. Corrosion

    b. Ovality

    c. Lamination & seams and mechanical damages

    d. All of the above

5. Which of the following are influenced by fabricating procedure that calls for fillet welds to be 'blended in' by grinding?

    a. HAZ cracking

    b. Fatigue life

    c. Residual stress

    d. Yield strength

6. The main reason for pre-heating medium and high carbon steels before cutting by oxy-fuel gas technique is to,

    a. Improve the quality of the cut

    b. Increase the cutting speed

    c. Refine the grain structure

    d. Prevent hardening and cracking

7. What is the advantage of low carbon electrode and plate material for welding austenitic stainless steel?

    a. Prevent cracking in the heat affected zone

    b. The formation of chromium carbides

    c. Prevent cracking in the weld metal

    d. Prevent distortion

8. Which one of the following does NOT minimize angular distortion during welding?

    a. Use of double 'V' weld prep using balanced welding technique.

    b. Pre-setting of work piece by using fixations and clamps.

    c. Applying post weld heat soak.

    d. Changing from a single 'V' prep for thick material.

9. Which of the following is required before starting?

    a. Prequalified or qualified welding procedure WPS

    b. Procedure qualification record PQR

    c. Welders' performance qualification records

    d. All of the above

10. Which of the following are inputs to the oxy-fuel cutting torch?

    a. The fuel gas like acetylene

    b. Preheated oxygen

    c. Cutting oxygen

    d. All of the above

11. Which of the following materials are cut using the traditional oxy-fuel cutting process?

    a. Aluminum alloys

    b. Stainless steel alloys

    c. Carbon and low alloy steel

    d. Copper alloys

12. Which of the following cutting processes is used in back gouging welds or to remove defective welds to prepare for repair work?

    a. Plasma arc cutting PAC

    b. Oxy-fuel cutting OFC

    c. Air carbon arc cutting CAC-A

    d. All of the above

13. Which of the following mechanical cutting processes are used in the fabrication of welding components?

    a. Grinding

    b. Sawing

    c. Drilling

    d. All of the above

14. Which of the following describe the joint and weld below?

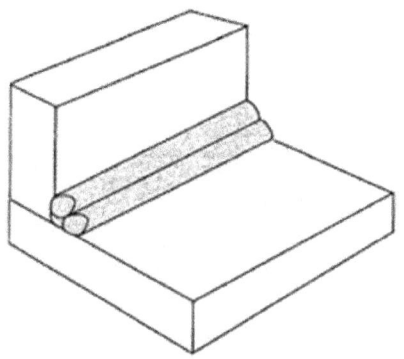

I Corner joint
II Equal leg Fillet weld
III Unequal leg fillet weld
IV None of the above

a. I & II
b. I & III
c. II & III
d. II & IV

15. Which of the following describe the weld below?

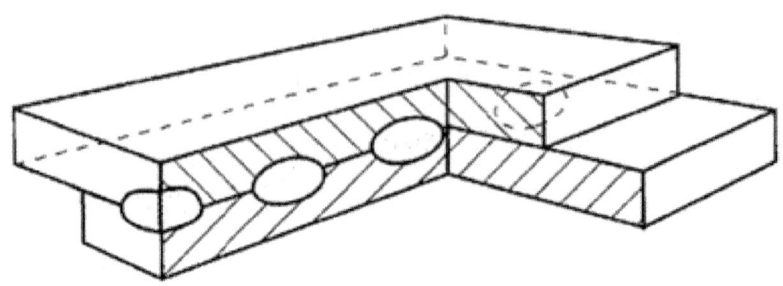

a. Slot weld
b. Resistance spot weld
c. Plug weld
d. None of the above

16. Which of the following welding symbols express the weld below?

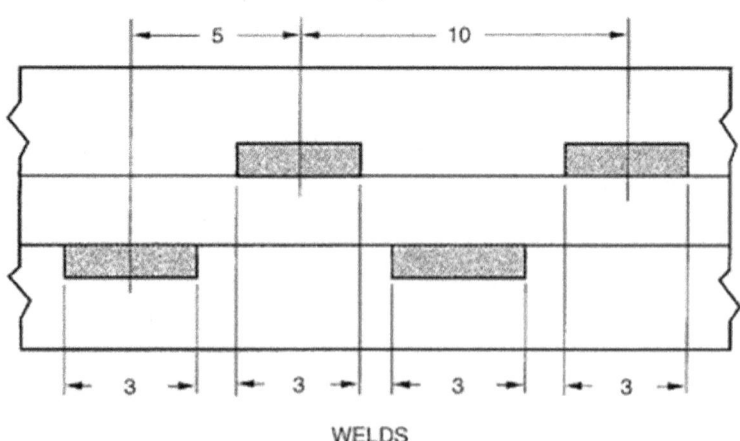

WELDS

a.

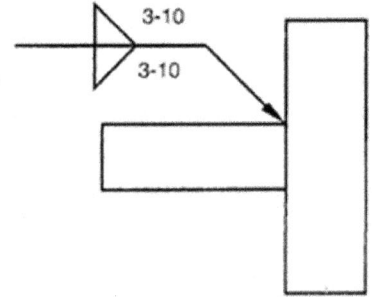

b.

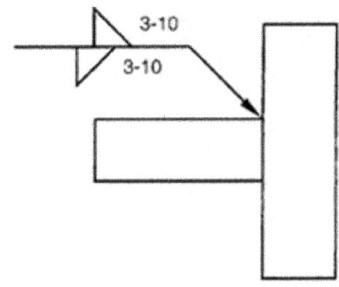

c. Both a & b
d. Neither a or b

17. Which of the following symbols is matching the below projected weld cross section?

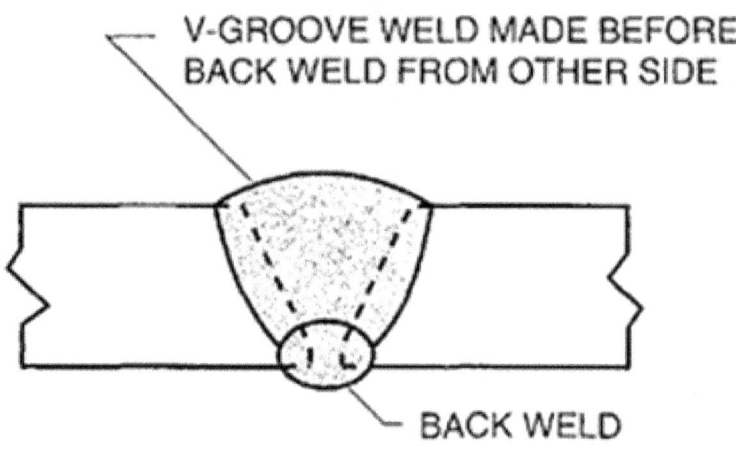

WELD CROSS SECTION

a.

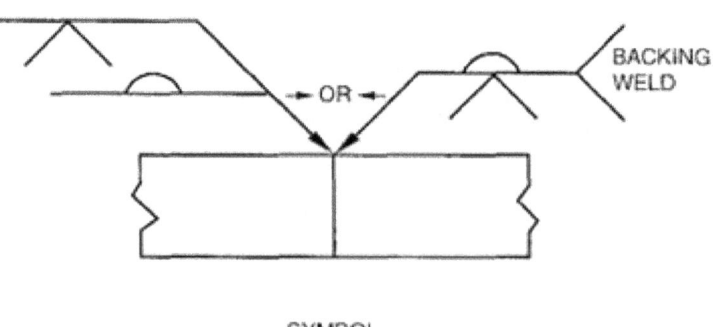

SYMBOL

b.

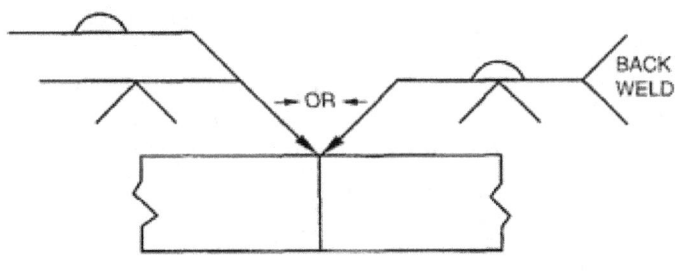

SYMBOL

c. Neither of the above
d. Both of the above

18. Tolerances on drawings of welding components can be expressed,

a. As variations between limits
b. As the design size followed by the tolerance
c. When only one value is given, the other value is assumed to be zero
d. All of the above

19. Which of the following standards is the most common in steel structure design and fabrication:

a. AWS D1.1
b. AWS D1.2
c. AWS D1.3
d. AWS D1.4

20. What is meant by a pre qualified welding procedure?

a. A welding procedure which is qualified in the previous project

b. Welding procedures which have some limitations defined by the standard committee and can be used without procedure qualification or PQR.

c. Welding procedure that is qualified by other material in the same material group.

d. None of the above

21. Which of the following standards is concerned with un-fired pressure vessels design and fabrication?

a. ASME I
b. ASME II
c. ASME IX
d. ASME VIII

22. Which of the following welding processes is used for welding sheet metals in automotive and aerospace industries?

a. Shield metal arc welding
b. Gas tungsten arc welding
c. Thermit welding
d. Resistance welding

23. Which of the following is/are surface preparation methods?

a. sand blasting
b. ball blasting
c. Both
d. none

24. Which of the following is/are surface finishing methods?

   a. Grinding
   b. Brushing
   c. Both of the above
   d. None of the above

25. Which of the following is/are surface fabricated structures?

   a. Bridge
   b. Pressure vessels
   c. Both
   d. None of the above

Answer Key

1. C
Weldability of metals does not depend on the boiling point as at this point, the material transfers to vapor. Choice A, melting point, is very important as it determines the amount of thermal energy required to fuse the material. Choice D, thermal conductivity, determines the ability of materials to keep the arc energy without diffusion, so it is important in material weldability. Choice B, thermal expansion of materials is important as it determines the amount of distortion after welding and the retained stresses in welded joints.

2. B
Square butt joints are a joint where the two base metals to be welded are put together face to face. This is very common in welding thin sheets. A double flare butt joint is a joint between two rebars or rods, which are put together length-wise and form a flare groove which does not need any preparation.

Choice A, single vee, and single bevel groove butt joints, (choice C) need the base metal bevelled at certain angles.

3. D
All the choices should be included in your inspection.

4. D
All of these factors should be inspected, including the condition of the material, corrosion, diameter ovality, presence of lamination and any mechanical damage marks.

5. B
Fatigue life depends on the quality of the weld which should be smooth, free of notches or sharp transitions, and blended in. This will prevent cracks and propagation under load.

6. D
Preheating base metal before cutting and welding will decrease the cooling and material hardening, distortion and cracking, especially for material that is liable to hardening such as medium and high carbon steels.

7. B
Welding stainless steel requires low carbon content for both the base metal and the filler metal to avoid sensitization. This occurs with the formation of chromium carbides in heat affected zones and weld metal, so the free chromium available in the material after sensitization is lower than the protection limit (10.4%Cr) that enables the material to resist corrosion.

8. C
Angular distortion can be decreased by using double-vee joint preparation, usage of joint pre-setting. Applying post weld heat soaking will relieve the welding stresses and enhance material structure.

9. D
Before starting, you should have an approved welding procedure including joint preparation, welding process to be used, required preheat, filler materials to be used, approved materials to be welded, post weld heat treatment if required, welding techniques to be followed, cleaning and grinding techniques to be followed and welding parameters of current, voltage and travel speed to be followed.

Also, a PQR is required for the materials that you do not have previous qualification for, so the welding engineer perform the required tests to validate the proposed welding procedure. If the results are ok, a record is approved and the WPS is generated from the approved PQR.

10. D
All of the choices are correct. There are three inputs: first, the fuel gas, like acetylene, methane (natural gas), propane, gasoline and methylacetylene - propadiene (MPS). Second, the preheated oxygen which is responsible for heating the area to be cut to the kindling temperature, For steel, the kindling temperature is 925 C. Third, after reaching the kindling temperature, the cutting oxygen is allowed to flow to start the cutting process by oxidizing the preheated steel leading to an exothermic reaction, which produces thermal energy sufficient to melt and cut.

11. C
Only carbon and low alloy steel can be cut with an oxy-fuel cutting process.

Criteria of traditional oxy-fuel cutting processes includes

- The material must have the capability of burning in a stream of oxygen.
- The materials ignition temperature must be lower than its melting temperature.
- Its heat conductivity should be relatively low. [not applicable for copper or aluminum]
- The metal oxide produced must melt at a temperature below the melting point of the metal. [not applicable for aluminum]
- The formed slag must be of low viscosity. [not applicable for copper, aluminum and stainless steel].

12. C
Air carbon arc cutting is used to back gouge welds to prepare the joint to weld from the other side. This is a very common procedure in steel structure fabrication. This process uses a carbon or graphite electrode to create an arc for heating, along with a stream of high pressure compressed air to mechanically remove the molten metal. This process can be used with many types of materials including carbon steels, stainless steels, aluminum alloys, magnesium alloys, cast iron, copper alloys and nickel-based alloys.

13. D
All of the choices are used in preparing components to be welded whether by grinding, sawing, drilling, shearing, milling or chipping.

14. A
I & II
This joint is a corner joint and welded with equal leg fillet weld.

15. B
This is a resistance spot weld in which the two overlapping pieces are welded at the faying surface between them where

the welding heat is created by resistance. Plug and slot welding occurs by drilling plugs or slots.

16. B

The projected weld is a staggered fillet weld where the length of weld is 3" and the center distance between the welds is 10". Choice A is for a chain fillet weld as shown below:

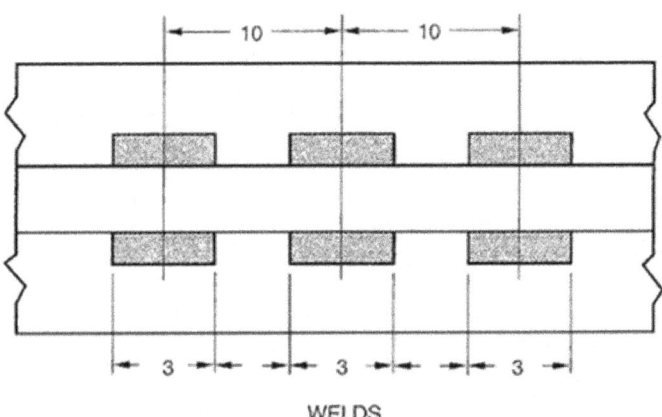

WELDS

17. B

The second symbol is correct as the welding is done first in the vee groove, and then back gouging, and finally welded from the back side.

18. B

All of the above are correct as shown below:

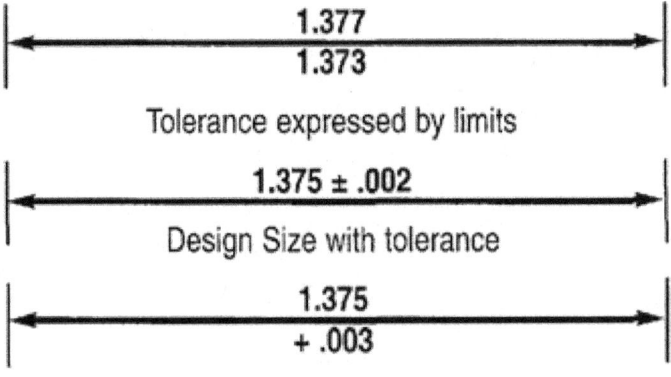

19. A
AWS D1.1 is the common standard used all over the world in designing and fabricating steel structures.
AWS D1.2 is the structural welding code for aluminum, AWS D1.3 is the structural welding code for sheet steel and AWS D1.4 is the structural welding code for reinforcing steel.

20. B
Pre qualified welding procedures are designed by the standards committee for common materials. The committee places limitations on pre qualified welding procedures to decrease the number of procedures requiring qualifications.

Procedures such as AWS D1.1 specify the joint preparations, preheat requirements and recommended filler materials

21. D
ASME VIII gives the rules for construction of pressure vessels.
ASME I gives the rules for construction of power boilers.
ASME II gives complete information about materials.
ASME IX gives rules of welding and brazing qualifications.

22. D
Resistance welding is a common welding procedure in the automotive industry, as it is used with thin sheet metal and resistance between two copper electrodes, with the current flowing between the electrodes to weld overlapping sheets.

23. C
Before painting, the material's surface is prepared by sand blasting and ball blasting to remove rust, grime or paint. Each paint requires certain surface roughness which is called the anchor profile.

24. C
Surface finishing is performed after welding whether by grinding to remove any visual defects like spatter, surface porosity and any extra welds. Wire brushes are used for surface finishing to remove rust, and also used before welding to clean the area.

25. C
Bridges and pressure vessels are structures that are fabricated using welding.

WELDING PROCESSES

The Welding Processes section includes:

- Questions on the use of shielded metal arc welding processes
- Questions on the use of gas metal arc welding, metal cored arc welding, and flux cored arc welding processes.
- Questions on gas tungsten arc welding processes.
- Questions on the process of submerged arc welding.

Answer Sheet

1. (A) (B) (C) (D)   11. (A) (B) (C) (D)   21. (A) (B) (C) (D)
2. (A) (B) (C) (D)   12. (A) (B) (C) (D)   22. (A) (B) (C) (D)
3. (A) (B) (C) (D)   13. (A) (B) (C) (D)   23. (A) (B) (C) (D)
4. (A) (B) (C) (D)   14. (A) (B) (C) (D)   24. (A) (B) (C) (D)
5. (A) (B) (C) (D)   15. (A) (B) (C) (D)   25. (A) (B) (C) (D)
6. (A) (B) (C) (D)   16. (A) (B) (C) (D)
7. (A) (B) (C) (D)   17. (A) (B) (C) (D)
8. (A) (B) (C) (D)   18. (A) (B) (C) (D)
9. (A) (B) (C) (D)   19. (A) (B) (C) (D)
10. (A) (B) (C) (D)   20. (A) (B) (C) (D)

SHIELDED METAL AND GAS METAL ARC WELDING

1. Which component below is not a part of shielded metal arc welding process?

    a. Flux coated electrode

    b. Argon gas

    c. DC/AC supply

    d. Base metal

2. What is shielded metal arc welding used for?

    a. Ideal for site work

    b. Pressure vessel

    c. Piping work

    d. All of the above

3. Which of the following is NOT an advantage of SMAW process?

    a. Ideal for site work

    b. High Instrument Cost

    c. Low Maintenance cost

    d. All of the above

4. Which of the following is a limitation of SMAW process?

    a. Lower deposition rate

    b. Higher current

    c. Low operator duty cycle

    d. Chipping slag

    e. All of the above

5. Which of the following is equipment for manual arc welding?

    a. Transformer rectifier

    b. Electrode hand piece and lead

    c. Work return lead

    d. All of the above

6. Which of the following is NOT a variable in SMAW processes?

    a. Ampere

    b. Arc voltage

    c. Travel speed

    d. Angle of approach

7. Undercut defects are due to

    a. Excessive amperage

    b. Incorrect arc length (too long)

    c. Incorrect electrode angle

    d. All of the above

8. Slag inclusion is due to

    a. Low ampere

    b. Incorrect joint preparation

    c. Dirty welding environment

    d. All of the above

9. Which of the following are defects due to the wrong angle of approach?

    a. Slag inclusion
    b. Lack of fusion
    c. Unacceptable weld contour
    d. All of the above

10. According to ISO 2560B, (welding electrode code) what do the last two digit represent?

    a. Tensile strength of deposited weld
    b. Type of flux
    c. Type of electrode
    d. None of the above

11. Which of the following is NOT a part of submerged arc welding (SAW)?

    a. Granular flux
    b. Electrode
    c. Shielding gas
    d. Base metal

12. Which of the following is an advantage of SAW process?

    a. Plate up to 75 mm thick welded in one pass
    b. Can use multiple wires simultaneously
    c. Thin material up to 2.1 mm can be welded
    d. All of the above

13. Which of the following is a limitation of SAW process?

a. Not suitable for positional welding
b. Exclusive use on low-alloy
c. High heat input
d. All of the above

14. Which of the choices below is/are equipment used in SAW?

a. Flux hopper
b. Auto torch
c. Electrode lead
d. Welding wire
e. All of the above

15. Which is the effect of voltage variation in SAW ?

a. High arc voltage gives a wider weld with less penetration
b. Low arc voltage causes a rough, irregular and narrow weld bead
c. Low voltage causes gas holes and craters
d. All of the above

16. Which of the following is/are variable(s) affecting the SAW process?

a. Arc voltage
b. Feed rate for wire
c. Types and quality of flux
d. Travel rate
e. All of the above

17. Which of the following causes cracking in SAW process?

    a. Low weld ability of steel
    b. Low temperature and fast cooling rate
    c. Polarity
    d. Internal shrinkage
    e. All of the above

18. What causes an excessive penetration defect in SMAW processes?

    a. Incorrect joint preparation
    b. Incorrect electrode choice
    c. Excessive ampere
    d. All of the above

19. What causes porosity defects in SMAW processes?

    a. Too long an arc
    b. Moist work material
    c. Too much current
    d. All of the above

20. Which of the following is NOT a type of cracking that occurs in SMAW processes?

    a. Hot cracking
    b. Cold cracking
    c. Cavity cracking
    d. Craters crack

21. What polarity do electrodes connect in GMAW welding wire?

    a. Direct Current (+).

    b. Direct Current (-).

    c. Alternative Current.

    d. All of the Above.

22. What is a major advantage of pulsed spray transfer?

    a. Increased amount distortion

    b. Low deposition rates with increased spatter

    c. Increased heat input compared to spray transfer

    d. All position welding on thinner material

23. Which parameter increases the width of a weld bead in GMAW?

1)   Increase in voltage
2)   Decrease in voltage
3)   Increase in speed
4)   Decrease in Speed

    a. 1 & 2

    b. 2 & 3

    c. 1 & 4

    d. 1 only

24. What is an appropriate angle of travel for the torch?

    a. $10° - 30°$

    b. $45° - 90°$

    c. $30° - 60°$

    d. $0° - 10°$

25. For deep penetration and high heat, which gas is used as a shielding gas in GMAW?

    a. Argon
    b. CO_2
    c. O_2
    d. $Ar + CO_2$

Answer Key

1. A
Argon Gas

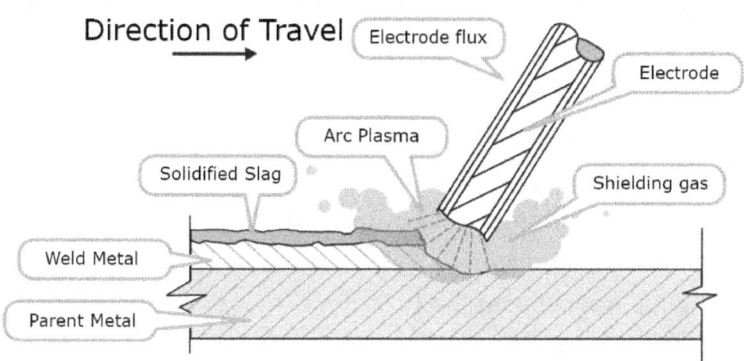

2. D
All of the above.

SMAW is widely used for:

- Structural work
- Pressure vessels
- Piping
- Maintenance
- Welding site construction
- General fabrication

3. B
High instrument cost

The advantage of the SMAW is its versatility and the availability of a wide range of supplies. Set-up time is quick, and perfect for small jobs, short production runs, and on-site welding.

MMAW offers the following advantages over other welding processes:

- low equipment cost
- versatility across a wide range of applications
- simple, reliable equipment
- low maintenance of equipment
- ideal for site work
- wide operator appeal
- sound, reliable welds.

4. E
All of the above

5. D
All of the above.

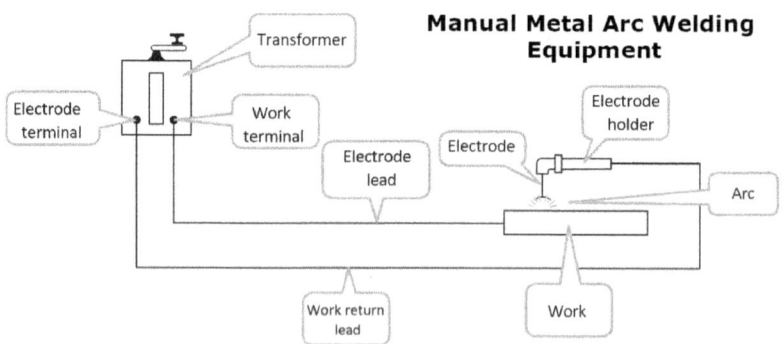

6. B
Arc Voltage is NOT a variable for SMAW process
Arc voltage is not considered to be a variable in the MMAW process as it is dependent on the electrode flux type and only varies from around 21 – 25 volts.

The major variables of the MMAW process are:

- amperage
- arc length
- travel speed
- angle of approach
- angle of travel

7. D
All of the above.

Undercuts are grooves or channels that can occur

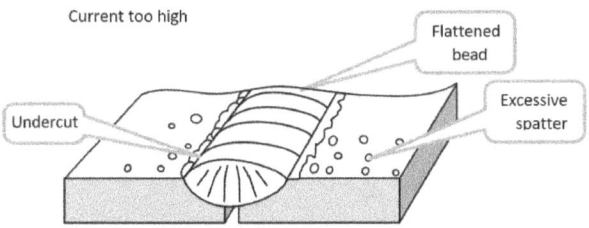

8. D
All of the above.

Slag inclusions can occur at the weld root; between weld runs, or on the weld surface. Low amperage, poor electrode manipulation, dirty or contaminated metal, or incorrect joint preparation all cause slag inclusion.

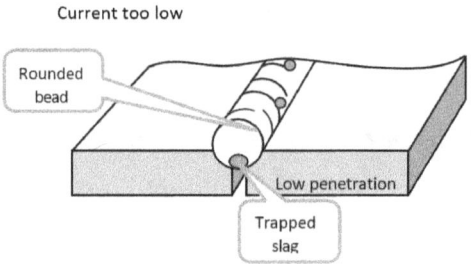

9. D

All of the above are defects due to the wrong angle of approach.

For an even weld, when the plates are at right angles, the electrode must be at 45°, evenly between both plates.

Incorrect angle can cause:

- slag inclusions
- lack of fusion and penetration
- unusual or unacceptable weld contours

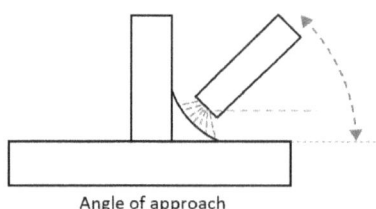

Angle of approach

MMAW common defects are:

- weld cracking
- contour faults
- lack of fusion
- stray arcing

- excessive or insufficient penetration
- excessive spatter
- slag inclusions
- undercut
- porosity

10. B
The last two digits are the type of flux.

11. C
Shielding gas.

In SAW, a layer of fine mineral or flux covers the weld. Flux is very conductive and fuses, forming an airtight slag, which slows cooling by protecting the molten metal from nitrogen and oxygen.

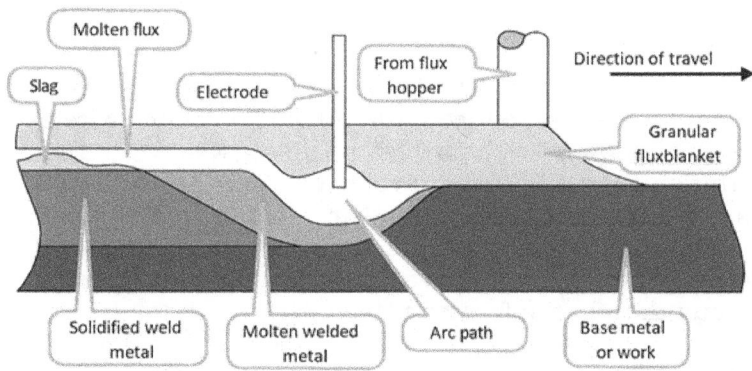

12. D
All of the choices are advantages of the SAW process

13. D
All of the above

14. E
All of the choices are equipment used in SAW.

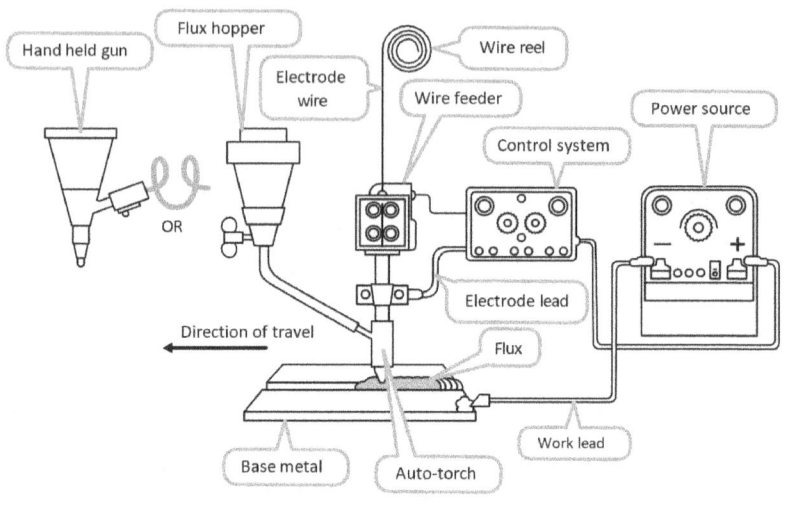

15. D
All of the above.

As the arc voltage is reduced, the tip of the welding wires operates at a lower level, giving a narrower weld with deeper penetration than a higher arc voltage under the same conditions. With high arc voltage, the wire tip operates at a high level, allowing the metal to spread out, giving a wider weld with less penetration. It also allows the fusing of slightly more flux than in the former case.

An extremely low arc voltage the molten deposited metal is forced up around the sides and to the rear of the crater. The bead will therefore, be rough, irregular, and comparatively high and narrow, sometimes with visible gas holes. With an excessively high arc voltage under the same current conditions, the tip of the welding wire high above the plate surface, the covering flux will tend to extinguish the arc. The resultant bead will be rough and irregular, flat and wide.

16. E
All of the choices are variables affecting the SAW process.

17. E
All of the choices can cause cracking in the SAW process.

18. D
All of the choices can cause excessive penetration defect in SMAW processes.

19. D
All of the choices can cause porosity defects in SMAW processes.

Porosity in SMAW welds can be the result of

- metal such as steel that contains high amounts of dissolved gases or sulphur

- dirty material

- material contaminated with moisture, oil, paint or grease

- Contaminated electrodes

- too much current

- too long an arc length

20. C
Cavity cracking.

21. A
Direct Current.

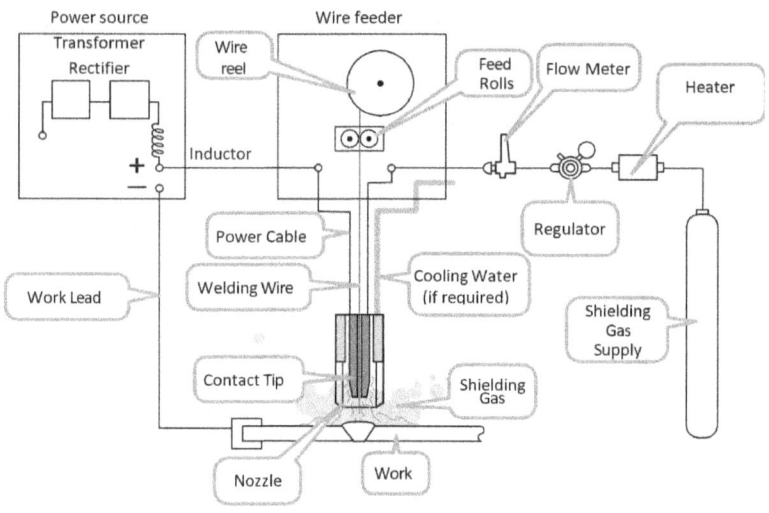

22. D
All position welding on thinner Material.

23. C
1 & 4 - Effect of Arc Voltage.
Voltage determines the mode of metal transfer in GMA welding. At low voltages, resistance extinguishes the arc, resulting in dip transfer. At higher voltages the arc by overcoming the electrical resistance. Arc length increases as voltage increases. At higher voltages, more wire is melted without 'stubbing,' which increases the width of the weld bead.

24. A
10^0 - 30^0
optimal angle is a trade-off between visibility and shielding. At low angles, shielding efficiency is reduced due to the Venturi effect, which draws air into the gas shield.
The Venturi effect is not present when making heavy welds, where the gun is 'dragged,' which directs shielding gas over the cooling weld.

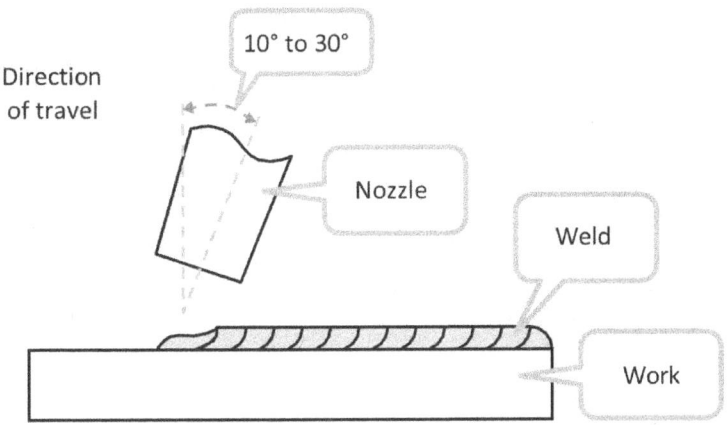

Nozzle Angle

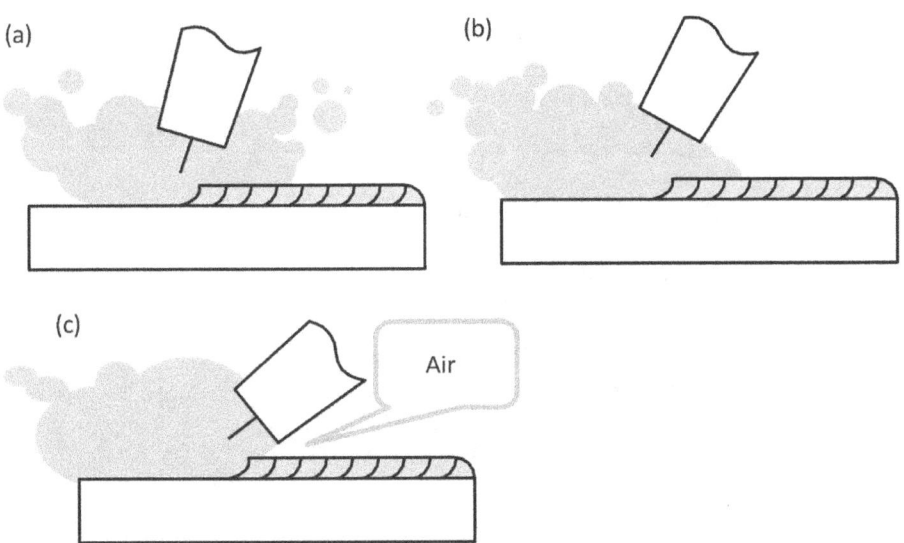

(a) Correct (b) incorrect (c) incorrect

25. B
CO_2

CO_2 is used as it has welding arc characteristics:

- deep penetration
- high spatter levels
- high deposition rates
- high heat input
- true spray transfer cannot be achieved.
- Produces convex bead shapes
- High spatter level

Argon
Argon is a true inert gas with the following characteristics:

- Smooth arc

- Used for non-ferrous metals

- Promotes spray transfer

- Cannot be used to weld carbon

- Cannot be used to weld low-alloy steel

- Lower heat input

- Lower penetration

- Lower spatter

- Improved bead shape

Gas Tungsten Arc Welding

Answer Key

1. (A) (B) (C) (D) 11. (A) (B) (C) (D) 21. (A) (B) (C) (D)
2. (A) (B) (C) (D) 12. (A) (B) (C) (D)
3. (A) (B) (C) (D) 13. (A) (B) (C) (D)
4. (A) (B) (C) (D) 14. (A) (B) (C) (D)
5. (A) (B) (C) (D) 15. (A) (B) (C) (D)
6. (A) (B) (C) (D) 16. (A) (B) (C) (D)
7. (A) (B) (C) (D) 17. (A) (B) (C) (D)
8. (A) (B) (C) (D) 18. (A) (B) (C) (D)
9. (A) (B) (C) (D) 19. (A) (B) (C) (D)
10. (A) (B) (C) (D) 20. (A) (B) (C) (D)

Gas Tungsten Arc Welding

1. What is meant by TIG (tungsten inert gas) autogenous welding?

    a. Welding with using pure tungsten electrodes

    b. Welding without using filler metals

    c. Welding in automotive factories

    d. Welding by using robots

2. What is the common type of shielding gases used in steel and stainless-steel welding?

    a. Argon

    b. Helium

    c. Carbon dioxide

    d. hydrogen

3. What is the tungsten electrode in TIG process is called?

    a. Consumable electrode

    b. Non-consumable electrode

    c. Low hydrogen electrode

    d. Cellulosic electrode

4. What is the common welding electrode polarity used with steel welding?

    a. DCEP

    b. DCEN

    c. AC

    d. None of the above

5. Deep penetration is achieved when welding with:

   a. DCEP
   b. DCEN
   c. AC
   d. Pulsed current

6. What are the common techniques for starting the TIG arc?

   a. Lift arc and HF start.
   b. Arc ignition by increasing current
   c. None of the above

7. Which type of tungsten electrodes used with AC current?

   a. Tungsten thoriated
   b. Tungsten zirconated and lanthaniated
   c. Pure tungsten

8. Which type of tungsten electrodes used with steels and most metals?

   a. Tungsten thoriated and Ceriated
   b. Tungsten zirconated
   c. Pure tungsten
   d. None of the above

9. When TIG welding austenitic stainless-steel pipe, argon gas purging is used to:

   a. Prevent oxidation
   b. Prevent under bead cracking
   c. Prevent porosity
   d. Control the penetration bead shape

10. Which one of the following types of types of steel is liable to create porosity when autogenously welded with an arc process?

    a. Fully killed steel

    b. Semi killed steel

    c. Rimming steel

    d. Fine grained steel

11. What is meant by tungsten electrode stick out:

    a. The distance from gas nozzle tip to electrode tip

    b. The distance from contact tip to electrode tip

    c. The arc length

    d. None of the above

12. What will happen if the tungsten electrode extension is too large?

    a. Contamination of weld-metal by tungsten inclusions

    b. Unstable arc

    c. Deep penetration

    d. None of the above

13. What will happen if the tungsten electrode extension is too small?

    a. Contamination of weld-metal by tungsten inclusions

    b. Unstable arc

    c. Deep penetration

    d. None of the above

14. The color code of pure tungsten electrodes is _____ and the color code of tungsten 20% thoriated electrodes is _____.

   a. Red, yellow
   b. Green, red
   c. Grey, gold
   d. Yellow, red

15. Which of the following is correct regarding the vertex angle of tungsten electrode tip preparation for TIG using DCEN?

   I   With increasing the vertex angle, the penetration increases.
   II With increasing the vertex angle, the penetration decreases.
   III With decreasing the vertex angle, the bead width increases.
   IV With decreasing the vertex angle, the bead width decreases.

   a. I & II
   b. II & III
   c. I & III
   d. II & IV

16. What is the proper tungsten electrode tip preparation for TIG using AC current:

   a. Chamfering to moderate vertex angle.
   b. The electrode tip is chamfered and forms a ball end when welding.
   c. The electrode tip is not chamfered and left square as it is.
   d. None of the above.

17. Which of the following filler metals is used with TIG in welding carbon steel?

I ER70S-6
II E7018
III E71T-GS
IV ER70S-3

a. I & III
b. II & III
c. I & IV
d. III & IV

18. Which of the following tungsten electrodes & currents are used for TIG welding stainless steels and nickel-based alloys?

a. Tungsten thoriated, DCEP
b. Tungsten lanthaniated, DCEN
c. Tungsten ceriated, DCEN
d. Pure tungsten, AC

19. Which one of the following shielding gases produces the deepest penetration in TIG welding?

a. Helium
b. Argon
c. Co2
d. Oxygen

20. What is the normal flow rate of shielding gas used in TIG welding?

    a. 1-4 litre/minute

    b. 5-10 litre/minute

    c. 2-7 litre/minute

    d. 15-20 litre/minute

21. Why is AC is preferred for welding aluminum using TIG welding?

    a. It gives arc stability and cleaning action during welding

    b. It gives deep penetration

    c. To avoid weld cracks

    d. It gives good weld profile

Answer Key

1. B
Autogenous welding is a welding done by using TIG welding without any filler metals where the fusion of both metals to be welded is done by the arc of the non-consumable tungsten electrodes.

2. A
Argon is the most common shielding gas used with TIG welding process for carbon steel and stainless-steel materials. Helium is commonly used when welding non-ferrous metals especially thick ones.

3. B
In TIG welding, tungsten is a non-consumable electrode and its main function is to construct the welding arc with the workpiece. In other welding processes like SMAW, the welding electrodes are consumable ones which are mainly used to construct the welding arc in addition to filling the welding joint like the low hydrogen electrodes like E7018 and cellulosic electrodes like E6010.

4. B
The polarity used for steels is always DCEN, as most of the heat is concentrated at the DCEP pole. This is required to keep the tungsten electrode at the cool end of the arc. For welding aluminum, AC current is used to create the auto-cleaning action by continuous alteration of polarity to break the formed oxide layer of aluminum during welding.

5. B
High penetration is achieved by using DCEN as 70% of heat is concentrated at the work piece, while 30% at the electrode that occurs with DCEP. When using AC, moderate penetration is achieved as 50% of heat is concentrated at the workpiece and 50% at the electrode.

6. A
Lift arc occurs when the tungsten electrode touches the workpiece. This technique is not suitable when welding with AC. There is also the issue of contamination of weld metal

by tungsten inclusions caused by touching the work piece. HF start occurs by introducing high frequency current that enables the arc to start without touching the workpiece.

7. B
Tungsten zirconated is an old type which is slightly radioactive. The newer tungsten lanthaniated, is not radioactive like tungsten zirconated electrode.

8. A
Tungsten thoriated electrodes are used in welding steels and most metals with DCEN polarity.

9. A
Stainless steel welds are liable to oxidation from the root side due to the presence of oxide forming elements like chromium Cr, which, during welding with oxygen, will form chromium oxides Cr_2O_3. Welding stainless-steel, purging by inert gases like argon is required from the root side to prevent oxidation.

10. C
Rimmed steels are low carbon steel that is partially deoxidized or non-oxidized. They contain large amounts of oxygen, which upon welding will evolve out causing porosity.

11. A
Electrode Stick out distance is the distance from gas nozzle tip to electrode tip. The distance between contact tip to electrode tip is called electrode extension which usually is in the range 2-3 times the electrode diameter.

12. A
Tungsten electrode extension is the distance between welding torch contact tip and electrode tip and is usually in the range of 2-3 times the electrode diameter. If the extension is too large, the electrode will overheat, leading to deterioration of the weld metal by tungsten inclusions.

13. B

Tungsten electrode extension is the distance between welding torch contact tip and electrode tip and is usually in the range of 2-3 times the electrode diameter. If the extension is too small, it will result in lower emission of electrons leading to an unstable arc.

14. B

According to AWS 5.12, the color code for pure tungsten electrodes is green.

15. B

I & III

For TIG welding using DCEN, the tungsten electrode tip is prepared by chamfering the tip by grinder to an angle called the vertex angle. Increasing the vertex angle, increases the penetration due to the high intensity of the arc. Decreasing the vertex angle, the arc becomes wider leading to wide beads.

16. B

In TIG welding using AC current, the electrode tip is chamfered and forms a ball end due to the alternative change in polarity.

17. C

I & IV

Both ER70S-6 and ER70S-3 are used in welding carbon steel for single and multi-pass welding. They have different in chemical composition of alloying elements: ER70S-6 contains a higher content of manganese and silicon, so they can weld on base metal with light to moderate amounts of rust and mill scales.

18. C

Tungsten ceriated electrodes give improved arc stability and enhanced arc start, lower electrodes burn off compared to pure tungsten electrodes. in addition to the non-radioactivity aspect, they can replace tungsten thoriated electrodes using DCEN.

19. C
The higher arc strength of TIG with argon gives the deepest penetration of welds. Argon is the most common shielding gas used with TIG. Helium is used to produce hot arc with higher thermal energy suitable for welding thick nonferrous materials with high thermal conductivity like aluminum and copper alloys. Co2 and oxygen are used in mixes with argon and/or Helium for special purposes.

20. C
As a recommended practice in TIG welding, the usual flow rate is in the range 2-7 litre/minute range.

21. A
Aluminum alloys have high tendency to form oxides with air during welding. This creates an oxide layer, characterized by a higher melting point, around 2 times that of the base metal. This layer hinders the proper completion of welding, however, with AC, there is an alternative change in polarity, which helps break down this layer and produces clean welds free from oxides.

Cutting and Gouging

Cutting and Gouging questions include:

- Five questions that require the use of tools and equipment for grinding and non-thermal cutting.

- Seven questions that test his or her ability to use the process of oxy-fuel gas cutting (OFC) for gouging and cutting.

- Five questions that test your ability to use the process of plasma arc cutting (PAC) in cutting and gouging.

- Four questions that test the ability to use the process of air carbon arc cutting (CAC-A) in cutting and gouging.

Answer Key

	A	B	C	D	E			A	B	C	D	E
1	○	○	○	○	○		21	○	○	○	○	○
2	○	○	○	○	○		22	○	○	○	○	○
3	○	○	○	○	○		23	○	○	○	○	○
4	○	○	○	○	○		24	○	○	○	○	○
5	○	○	○	○	○		25	○	○	○	○	○
6	○	○	○	○	○							
7	○	○	○	○	○							
8	○	○	○	○	○							
9	○	○	○	○	○							
10	○	○	○	○	○							
11	○	○	○	○	○							
12	○	○	○	○	○							
13	○	○	○	○	○							
14	○	○	○	○	○							
15	○	○	○	○	○							
16	○	○	○	○	○							
17	○	○	○	○	○							
18	○	○	○	○	○							
19	○	○	○	○	○							
20	○	○	○	○	○							

1. Air arc gouging is generally not used for,

   a. Non-Ferrous alloy
   b. High carbon steel
   c. Carbon or low alloy steel
   d. Aluminum

2. Which of the following is not a part of the air arc gouging process?

   a. Electrode
   b. Air valve and jet
   c. Electrical power jet
   d. Shielding gas

3. Air arc gouging electrodes are made from,

   a. Carbon
   b. Graphite
   c. Copper
   d. All of the above

4. Which parameter below determines the size of the arc gouging groove?

   a. Size of electrode
   b. Travel speed
   c. Current
   d. Electrode angle
   e. All of the above

5. **Which of the following are components of plasma arc gouging?**

   a. Power source
   b. Electrode
   c. Air/Gas supply unit
   d. Torch
   e. All of the above

6. **Which of the following is NOT a function of the power source in plasma arc cutting processes?**

   a. Converting DC to AC
   b. Converting AC to DC
   c. Controlling air flow
   d. Circuit breaker

7. **Which of the following is a component part of a plasma arc torch?**

   a. Swirling ring
   b. Nozzle
   c. Electrode
   d. All of the above

8. **What are plasma cutting electrodes made of?**

   a. Steel
   b. Graphite
   c. Carbon
   d. Copper and Hafnium

9. Which of the following methods can start an arc without contact between the nozzle and the work piece?

    a. High frequency starting methods

    b. Lift arc methods

    c. Power arc control methods

    d. All of the above

10. Which of the following are characteristics of plasma gas for plasma arc cutting?

    a. High ionization potential

    b. High thermal conductivity

    c. High heat energy

    d. All of the above

11. Which of the following grinding machines are used before and after welding?

    a. Hand grinder

    b. Bench grinder

    c. Floor stand grinder

    d. All of the above

12. Which of the following are used to cut the material?

    a. High speed circular saw

    b. Water jet cutting machine

    c. EDM Machine

    d. None of the above

13. What is a silicon carbide grinding blade generally used for grinding or cutting?

    a. Aluminum

    b. Steel

    c. Copper

    d. Cast iron

14. What type of blade is used for cutting thick steel?

    a. Aluminum

    b. Steel

    c. Titanium carbide

    d. Aluminum oxide

15. What is the recommended air pressure for air carbon arc gouging?

    a. 50 PSI

    b. 80 PSI

    c. 120 PSI

    d. 80 - 100 PSI

16. What controls the depth of groove in air carbon arc gouging?

    a. Size of the electrode

    b. Speed of torch travel

    c. Base metal type

    d. Current supply

17. Which process variable below effects the quality of groove and metal removal rate?

    a. Ampere
    b. Voltage
    c. Electrode extensions
    d. Travel speed

18. Which of the following are NOT positions for air carbon arc gouging?

    a. Flat gouging
    b. Horizontal gouging
    c. Vertical gouging
    d. Overhead gouging
    e. None of the above

19. What is the bevel angle for travelling in air arc gouging process?

    a. 35^0
    b. $18^0 - 70^0$
    c. 90^0
    d. None of the above

20. What is the travelling angle for pad washing in air arc gouging process?

    a. 35^0
    b. $15^0 - 70^0$
    c. 90^0
    d. None of the above

21. What does the size of cutting nozzle used in oxy-acetylene processes mainly depend on?

a) Thickness of metal to be cut
b) Purity of oxygen
c) Duration of cut
d) Type of cutting blow pipe

22. Why is the top edge is melted round, and the cut face smooth in gas cutting?

a) Extreme high cutting speed
b) Insufficient acetylene gas supply
c) The nozzle being held too high
d) Too much cutting oxygen pressure

23. How far should you turn the valve on an oxygen cylinder?

a) all the way
b) half way
c) 1/4 turn
d) 1/2 turn

24. Which gas is always turned on, or turned off first?

a) Fuel
b) Oxygen
c) Both at a time
d) None of the above

25. How should you cut a deeper groove by gouging?

a) Increase the angle
b) Decrease the angle
c) Keep the angle constant
d) None of the above

Answer Key

1. C
Air arc gouging is generally not used for carbon or low alloy steel

Air arc gouging melts metal with the arc and clears molten metal with compressed air. Air-arc gouging is suited for:

- alloy steels
- quenched and tempered steels
- other metals that flame gouging could damage

2. D
Shielding gas is not a part of the air arc gouging process.

3. D
All of the above.

Electrodes are made from a carbon and graphite alloy coated with copper. The copper coating provides electrical conductivity and reduce radiant heat. Sizes range from 4mm to 12 mm. Hollow electrodes are available.

4. E
All of the above.

Groove size is determined by:

- electrode size
- speed of travel
- current
- electrode angle

To make a deeper groove, increase the electrode angle beyond the standard 20°. To widen the groove, move the electrode sideways.

5. E
All of the choices are components of plasma arc gouging.

6. B
Converting DC to AC is NOT a function of the power source.

7. D
All of the above.

The plasma torch consists of five component parts,

- Drag shield
- Retaining cup
- Electrode
- Swirling ring
- Torch

8. D
Plasma cutting electrodes are made of copper and hafnium

The electrode in plasma arc cutting provides the cutting arc start. Copper electrodes have an insert hafnium core, which easily releases electrons and is resistant to oxygen.

9. A
High frequency starting methods can start without contact between the nozzle and the work piece.

The four stages of starting a high frequency arc without contact with the work piece.

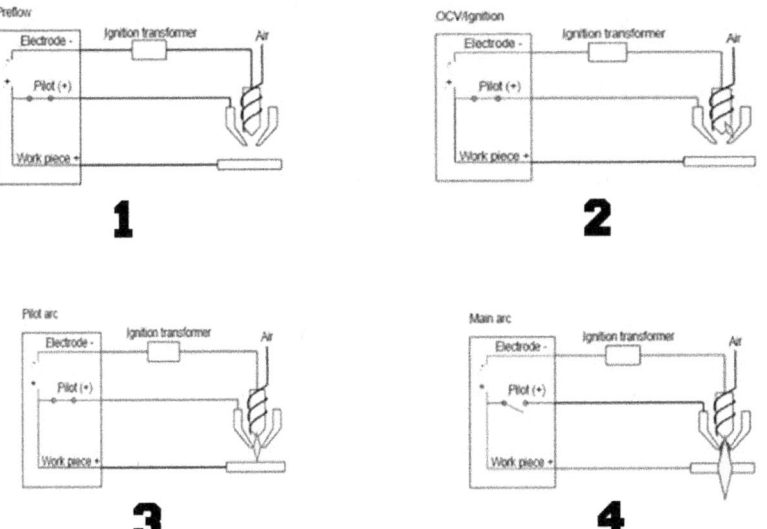

10. D
All of the choices are characteristics of plasma gas for plasma arc cutting.

To generate a good plasma arc, the plasma gas should have,

- Good thermal conductivity to transfer heat from the nozzle to the work piece
- High ionization for plasma generation
- High molecular weight to push out the cutting metal

11. D
All of the choices are used before and after welding.

There are four main types of rough grinders:

- Hand grinder
- Bench grinder
- Floor stands grinder
- Flexible shaft grinder

12. A
A high speed circular saw is used to cut the metal in welding shop.

13. D
A silicon carbide grinding blade generally used for grinding or cutting cast iron.

Grinding blades are made from two kind of material.

1) aluminum oxide, and
2) silicon carbide

Silicon carbide blades are used to cut brittle and hard material such as,

- Ceramic
- Glass
- Cast iron

Aluminum oxide blades are used for tough material such as,

- Stainless steel
- Low carbon steel

14. C
Titanium carbide blades are used for cutting thick steel.

15. D
80 - 100 PSI is the recommended air pressure for air carbon arc gouging.

Normal PSI for air carbon arc gouging ranges between 80 psi (551.6 kPa) and 100 psi (690 kPa) at the torch. Higher pressure does not increase efficiency. Lower pressure reduces the depth.

16. B
The depth of groove is controlled by the speed of torch travel.

The depth of groove is controlled by the travel speed, with fast travel speeds producing a shallow groove. The width of groove is controlled by the diameter of the electrode. Oscillating the electrode in a circular motion increases the groove width.

17. C
Electrode extensions effects the quality of groove and metal removal rate.

Variable	Effect
Amperage	Melts the base metal. Amperage depends on electrode size
Voltage	Controls arc length
Air pressure and rate of flow	For removing molten metal
Electrode extensions	Quality of groove and metal removal rate
Electrode size and work angle	Determines the groove shape

18. E
None of the choices are positions for air carbon arc gouging.

There are four different position for Air arc gouging process.

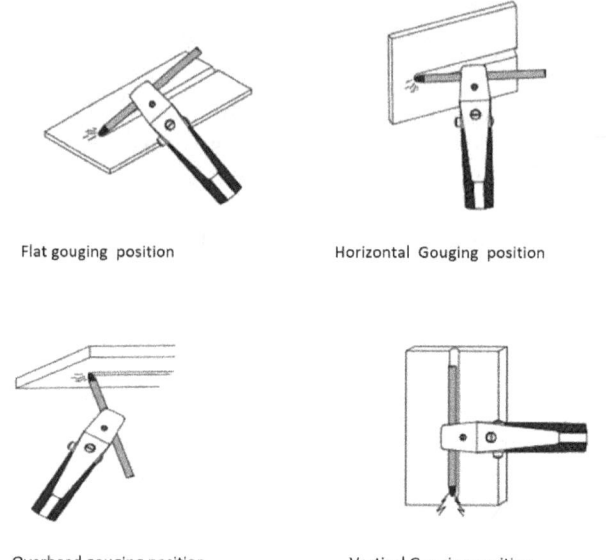

Flat gouging position   Horizontal Gouging position

Overhead gouging position   Vertical Gouging position.

19. C
$90°$ is the bevel angle for travelling in air arc gouging process.

20. B
$15° - 70°$
For removing metal from surfacing metal and riser pads on castings, wave the electrode from side-to-side while in a forward direction at the desired depth. In the pad-washing operation, use an angle of 15° to 70° to the work piece.

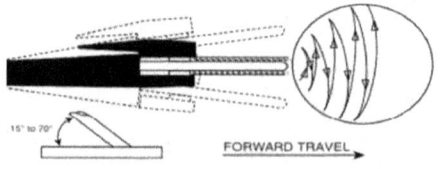

21. A

Thickness of metal to be cut.
The size of cutting nozzle and the pressure of gas depend on thickness of Material to be cut.

Thickness of Plate	Nozzle Size	Oxygen Pressure	Acetylene Pressure
3 mm	8	100 kPa	100 kPa
6 mm	8	180 kPa	100 kPa
12 mm	12	200 kPa	100 kPa
20 mm	12	235 kPa	100 kPa
25 mm	15	180 kPa	100 kPa
40 mm	15	300 kPa	100 kPa
50 mm	15	350 kPa	100 kPa

The first part of the type number gives the form of nozzle connection. The 30 series nozzles are a screw-in with a threaded inlet connection. The 40 series nozzles are the taper seat type. The second part of the type number indicates the fuel gas used. If the type number ends in a '1' the nozzle is used with acetylene, for example, type 41 nozzle is a taper seat nozzle for use with acetylene.

A type 44 nozzle is tapered for LPG. The LT type nozzle is for acetylene gas.

Gas number identification

1   Acetylene
2   Low pressure acetylene
3   Coal gas
4   LP gas
5   Hydrogen

Nozzle Size

The hole size number is stamped under the type number. The size number is in tenths of a millimeter, e.g. size 12 nozzle has a main bore diameter of 1.2 mm. Sizes for nozzles are 6, 8, 12, 15, 20, 24, 32 40, 48 and 64. Most common sizes for welding tips are 8, 10, 15, 20, 26, 32 and 38. Special nozzles other than standard, are identified by two letters after the size number.

DG	Deep gouging
TH	Heating tip
DS	Deseaming
PW	Power washing
FW	Flame washing
RC	Rivet cutting
GB	Gouging bent
RW	Rivet washing
GS	Gouging straight
SM	Sheet metal
HS	Hi-speed cutting
UW	Underwater

22. C
The nozzle being held to high
When the nozzle is too high, excessive rounding of the top edge occurs. Also, the cutting speed may have to be lowered. With the correct nozzle clearance, the preheat flames should not be more than 1/4" above the top surface of the plate.

Common faults in cutting and possible causes

Possible cause	Line of cut way or irregular (1)	Gouging of the cut way (2)	Top edge meted or rounded (3)	Undercut just below (4)	Bottom edge rounded, rougher irregular (5)	Cut tapered (6)	Pronounced lag or drag (7)	Excessive or tenacious slag (8)
Not enough preheat		■	■			■	■	
Too much Preheat		■	■					■
Cutting Oxygen pressure to law			■			■	■	
Cutting oxygen pressure too high			■	■		■		
Cutting speed too slow					■	■		■
Cutting speed too fast					■	■	■	
Bent magnet spindle or unsteady blow pipe	■							
Pre heat flame too high above work		■	■					
Pre heat Flame too close to work		■	■					■
Dirty nozzle	■	■	■	■	■	■	■	■
Dirty or rusty plate		■	■		■			
Nozzle to large								
Nozzle to small					■	■	■	

23. A
All the way.

The process of oxy-flame cutting makes use of the burning reaction between heated iron and oxygen. When iron is heated to above 815 °C (the ignition temperature) it readily combines with oxygen. The resulting reaction produces iron oxide. This reaction (combustion) also gives off extra heat which keeps the process of oxidation going.

The important point to note is that the reaction occurs at a lower temperature than the melting point of steel (approximately 1500 °C). The molten iron oxide together with some free iron, which runs off as molten slag, removed by the kinetic energy of an introduced jet of oxygen, thus exposing more preheated iron and iron oxide.

When a cutting attachment is fitted to a multi-purpose blowpipe, the blowpipe oxygen valve should be kept fully open at all times. Oxygen flow is then controlled via the preheat oxygen valve, and the cutting lever of the cutting attachment. Acetylene should be set to a 100 kPa maximum with the acetylene blowpipe valve open approximately one quarter of a turn.

24. A
Fuel

25. A
Increase angle of nozzle.
the angle and speed of the torch determines the depth of the gouge.

> **Deep grooves** - Increase the torch angle, which reduces the gouging speed, and increases the oxygen jet impingement angle.
>
> **Shallow grooves** - Decrease the torch angle, thereby increasing speed.
>
> **Wide grooves** can be produced by weaving the torch.
>
> **Nozzle size and parameters** effect the contour of the groove.

Low oxygen pressure - gouging leaves smooth ripples in the groove.

High oxygen pressure - gouging, especially in shallow grooves, is disrupted as the cut advances ahead of the molten pool.

Gouging Process and type
Flame gouging - Oxygen and a fuel gas create a high temperature flame. The steel is locally heated above the ignition temperature (9000 C). The resulting chemical reaction melts the metal.

Types of Gouging Processes

Progressive Gouging
Progressive gouging produces uniform grooves. Generally used to part-shape a steel forge, remove unfazed root areas on the reverse of a welded joint, remove a weld deposit and prepare plate edges for welding.

Spot Gouging
Spot gouging produces a deep narrow U-shaped groove. Generally used to remove localized areas like small imperfections. Gouging imperfections appear as light or dark spots or streaks in the molten pool.

Back-step Gouging
Back-step gouging is used to remove small imperfections. As the name implies, the torch backwards. The oxygen is shut off and the torch is then moved forward 25-30 mm before restarting the gouging operation.

Deep Gouging
Deep gouging combines progressive and spot gouging.

CONCLUSION

CONGRATULATIONS! You have made it this far because you have applied yourself diligently to practicing for the exam and no doubt improved your potential score considerably! Getting into a good school is a huge step in a journey that might be challenging at times but will be many times more rewarding and fulfilling. That is why being prepared is so important.

Study then Practice and then Succeed!

Good Luck!

https://www.facebook.com/CompleteTestPreparation/

https://www.youtube.com/user/MrTestPreparation

ONLINE RESOURCES

How to Prepare for a Test - The Ultimate Guide

https://www.test-preparation.ca/prepare-test/

Learning Styles - The Complete Guide

https://www.test-preparation.ca/learning-style/

Test Anxiety Secrets!

https://www.test-preparation.ca/test-anxiety/

Time Management on a Test

https://www.test-preparation.ca/time-management/

Flash Cards - The Complete Guide

https://www.test-preparation.ca/flash-cards/

Test Preparation Video Series

https://www.test-preparation.ca/test-video/

How to Memorize - The Complete Guide

https://www.test-preparation.ca/memorize/

Online Library of Student Tips and Strategies

https://www.test-preparation.ca/students-say/

www.ingramcontent.com/pod-product-compliance
Lightning Source LLC
LaVergne TN
LVHW010302260326
834688LV00044B/1420